Short St

The Bright Red Sports Car
and Other Stories

Study Guide

by Donald L. Deffner
Earl H. Gaulke, Editor

CONCORDIA PUBLISHING HOUSE • SAINT LOUIS

To
a very patient woman
my wife Corinne

Unless otherwise stated, Scripture taken from the HOLY BIBLE: NEW INTERNATIONAL VERSION®, © 1973, 1978, 1984 by International Bible Society. Used by permission of Zondervan Publishing House. All rights reserved.

The "NIV" and "New International Version" trademarks are registered in the United States Patent and Trademark Office by International Bible Society. Use of either trademark requires the permission of International Bible Society.

Quotations marked KJV are from the King James or Authorized Version of the Bible.

Scripture quotations marked NKJV are from the New King James edition, copyright © 1979, 1980, 1982. Used by permission.

The Bible text in this publication marked TEV is from the Good News Bible, the Bible in TODAY'S ENGLISH VERSION. Copyright © American Bible Society 1966, 1971, 1976. Used by permission.

Copyright © 1993 Concordia Publishing House
3558 South Jefferson Avenue, St. Louis, MO 63118-3968
Manufactured in the United States of America

All rights reserved. No part of this publication may be reproduced, stored in a retrieval system, or transmitted, in any form or by any means, electronic, mechanical, photocopying, recording, or otherwise, without prior written permission of Concordia Publishing House.

This publication is also available in braille or in large print for the visually impaired. Write to the Library for the Blind, 1333 South Kirkwood Road, St. Louis, MO 63122-7295. Allow at least one month for processing.

4 5 6 7 8 9 10 11   09 08 07 06 05 04 03 02

CONTENTS

About This Book   5

Session 1—Means of Grace   9
  "The Bright Red Sports Car"   9
  "The Listener"   15
  For Discussion   18

Session 2—Happiness   21
  "Old Man"   21
  "The Physician"   23
  For Discussion   27

Session 3—Grace/Thanksgiving   29
  "Appreciation"   29
  "Hello, Jan"   32
  For Discussion   35

Session 4—Loneliness   39
  "The Visit"   39
  "The Widow"   43
  For Discussion   48

Session 5—Aging   51
  "The Memory"   51
  For Discussion   61

Session 6—Death/Life   63
  "The Christmas Letter"   63
  For Discussion   69

Appendix 71
(For use as a follow-up to
"The Christmas Letter")

Acknowledgments 72

ABOUT THIS BOOK

Everyone loves a story!

In India a native evangelist has a bicycle, a lantern, and a drum. He goes into a village, people gather at the sound of the drum, and he tells them a story. It is the story of Jesus.

Jesus Himself told stories.

> Jesus used parables to tell all these things to the crowds; he would not say a thing to them without using a parable. (Matthew 13:34 TEV)

He would say, "A certain man was going down from Jerusalem to Jericho, when robbers attacked him . . ." (Luke 10:30). And a hearer mentally responded, *Yes, Rabbi, why I know just what you are talking about! Why, Uncle Daniel was attacked on that road just last week!*

Jesus followed the principle of going "from the known to the unknown." He started with the real world of his hearers and then moved on to the theological truth involved.

The apostle Paul used story, even quoting the secular literature of his day: "as even some of your poets have said . . ." (Acts 17:28).

Martin Luther wrote:

> Without knowledge of literature pure theology cannot at all endure . . . I see that there has never been a great revelation of the Word of God unless He has first prepared the way by the rise and prosperity of languages and letters, as though they were John the Baptists . . .

In *Theology and Modern Literature,* Amon Wilder held that in humanity's effort at self-understanding we need cultural images, works of art. Literature assists us in this search for self-understanding. "Philosophy and theology as rational disciplines are inadequate to the process." And Italian novelist Ignazio Silone in "The Choice of Companions" mused:

> The spiritual condition I have described allows of no boasting .... It resembles a camp of refugees in some no man's land, out in the open, existing by chance. What do you expect refugees to do from morning to night? They spend the best part of their time telling each other their stories. The stories are not very entertaining, to be sure, but they tell them anyhow—mainly, to understand what has happened.

Story is also receiving a revival in preaching today. Homiletician Charles Rice says, "The way towards renewal of preaching is to be found in the recovery of storytelling." Indeed, *the Bible is story*. Along with this has come an emphasis on the preacher's valid use (reflexive and self-insightful, not subjective) of "My Story" from the preacher's own faith-walk. This is then related to God's Story (the Gospel) and correlated with The People's Story—their own Christian life.

Children often say, "Tell me a story!" I believe I told my children the story about Hansel and Gretel one thousand times. They couldn't wait for the moment when the wicked witch would say, "And now I am going to throw you into my oven! *Boo!*" And then I would bundle them into my arms and hug them.

A seminary student recounts a class of junior high students he had. Bedlam reigned. The noise was intolerable. Then he said, "Say, I'd like to tell you a story." Suddenly silence fell over the group as they all settled down and listened attentively. He couldn't believe the change that had taken place, he said.

And stories also enliven adult Bible classes and home discussion groups. Our involvement in the characters' lives can quicken and enrich our concern for the issue involved—pride, gossip, loneliness, witnessing, etc.—and assist us as Christians in grappling with the question (as Francis Schaeffer puts it) "How should we then live?"

The following stories are offered as an issue-oriented resource for adult Bible study and discussion groups.

There are two 6-session courses, each session based on 1 to 3 short stories, arranged topically according to thematic issues, with discussion questions referencing Bible texts designed to lead the learner to apply Scripture to his/her own life. These are for use with small home-discussion groups or in the Sunday morning or weekday Bible class. Additionally, the study booklets can simply be used by individuals—for their own individual reading, meditation, and spiritual nourishment.

Because the story/stories for each session can be read in an average of 9 minutes (range, 5 to 13 minutes), the stories may be read at the time of meeting—either silently by each participant before discussion or orally by volunteer readers in the group. A third alternative is that the stories be read beforehand.

Also, the stories can be shared with people outside the church as a contact point for dialog in evangelization. Note the Appendix, which can be used as a discussion starter for "The Christmas Letter."

Indeed, "tell me *your* story" can be a fruitful catalyst in reaching out to others as we first *actively listen* to *them*. But then something else may occur. As J. Russell Hale, author of *Who Are the Unchurched,* says,

> Your tone of voice, gestures, etc., are very important as you say, "I'd like to have you tell me your story about what you think of the church. Go back to your childhood." *And they really open up.*
>
> If you listen when they tell you their story, a point will come when they'll say, "Tell me your story." And you don't hand out tracts, but as the two stories converge there is the miracle of dialog, the point when *God's story* can come out . . . And the "rumor of angels" impinges on their ordinary experiences.

In whatever setting you use this book, may the Holy Spirit attend your reading. And then, may you be moved to share with others *The Story.*

Besides the specific questions added after each story, here are some key questions to consider throughout the sessions:

1. Is the story true to life? Give reasons for your answer.

2. What, if anything, does the story have to say to our Christian faith and life?
3. How does it reveal or point to our need? (Law)
4. How does it point to or suggest God's action for us in Christ? (Gospel)

SESSION 1
Means of Grace

The Bright Red Sports Car

The red Mercedes sped along through the North Dakota countryside. Here and there the gently rolling hills were dotted with small ponds and lakes, real-life versions of small mirrors used in kindergarten table settings depicting rural winter scenes.

Carol maneuvered the sleek machine deftly down the highway and through the picturesque tableau. Spotted against the whiteness of the snow, the Mercedes seemed to cut a swath of color through the setting, streak of red on white, then on quickly to another scene up ahead, up ahead.

The car and the girl seemed to be one. Young, trim, and light of figure, Carol infused the Mercedes with a quality of her own. She gave it life and spirit, and it responded to her touch as if it were a part of her very own being.

Musing on the turned pages of her life and on the pages still ahead, Carol's brow tightened a little in pensive thought.

Back on campus in Iowa, the psychology prof had made things so *clear* and so *reasonable* to her. The old life she had had—centered in so many things at church—seemed distant and irrelevant to her now. For the first time she felt she could really show Mom and Dad why she had come to feel the way she did. The old "chestnuts"—one of her church friends had called them—came back to mind again. Questions she couldn't dismiss lightly without *thinking* about

them. And her roommate, Robin, had asked her the same questions in a hundred different ways over and over again!

"If God did make everything, then didn't He create evil, too?" "How can a loving God let innocent people suffer?" "If God *really* loves His creatures, why doesn't He show Himself more clearly and make His help more easily available to people?"

The Mercedes rolled on, and a small town appeared, then fell back in the distance as the car quickly left the scene and went on to another. In the yard of a farm by the side of the road was a stately old funeral coach, rusting and rotting in a shed. Inside the square glass windows, the heavy black drapes still hung in precise folds as if painted into position.

Thoughts of the coming reunion with the folks in the next town ahead flashed across her mind. And the car almost quickened in response and leaped ahead.

The folks—and Beth! Younger sister Beth. How they used to quarrel! Now it was so different, being away at school. She really missed her. A guilty feeling swept over Carol, remembering Beth's illness. Some internal complication, the doctor had said. The folks had not written very much about it.

But at the moment Carol couldn't deny the joy-to-be-alive mood that pulsed through her, the car, and the scenes all around that became more familiar by the mile. With a mental frown she rebelled against the idea of sickness or sorrow or pain. Everything seemed so good—so "right": the oneness with the car—the cool air brushing her cheek through the barely open window, the white ribbon of the pavement meanwhile being wound up into the motor of the car, as it were, like a vast, long hose stretching into the distance ahead.

The Mercedes was *her*. And as she pressed the accelerator, it was like a lover's hand, responding in answer to the pressure of love.

The well-known, well-loved blocks of her small home town flicked by in rapid, photolike succession, and suddenly she was in the driveway and, forgetting her young womanhood, bounding up on the porch, on the old boards which echoed with the familiar thud of her feet, inside the screen door, and into the arms of Mom and Dad.

But there was a shadow on Mom's face, a "nonverbal cue" the prof would have called it, which she sensed in the greeting. Something was wrong—Mother's whole body was like a bow with its string drawn taut and tense.

And then she knew: Beth was worse—she had a few weeks to live—it had all happened so fast—and they hadn't called her because they just found out a few days before—and since Carol couldn't do anything about it anyway, they might as well let her finish her pre-Christmas exams.

Slowly the crushing news hit her like a powerful fist smashing her on the forehead right above the eyes. Suddenly Carol felt guilt, yet rebellion. Death was a lie! It didn't fit! It was *wrong*. "I will not accept it." The words framed themselves in block letters in her mind.

In a few moments she was in Beth's bedroom. The embrace was warm and close, but somehow she seemed a stranger to her. Beth seemed so far away. Not in what she said—her smile and eyes were warm with happiness at seeing Carol. But there seemed to be something between them that hadn't been there before. And it was as if a strange presence of some mood or feeling filled the room, yet it was silent and still except for their talking.

And when Carol left after a few minutes—Mother had said the first visit should be a short one so as not to tax Beth's strength—Carol realized in a flash that *she* had done all the talking. Beth had been so happy for her. Really Carol had talked only about herself. And with a strange quirk of memory she also realized that she had really said none of the things she had planned to say to Mom and Dad about her feelings at school.

And then it happened. The day after Christmas—the hemorrhage—taking Beth back to the hospital—the funeral—living several days of sheer existence as she had never known life before—then a week of wandering around the house like a hollowed-out shell—or like the driver of a car, in shock after a highway accident, walking aimlessly in a field, walking and walking, but with no destination.

Back at school, with the new quarter begun, it all seemed like a nightmare. Carol could still see Beth coughing blood. "There's my life going down the drain," she had said, yet not bitterly, or with despair.

And as the psych prof lectured in the 10 A.M. section, Carol still felt many of the old doubts and questions recurring.

But now, somehow, these didn't seem to be the questions. What puzzled her was how Beth could have been so strong in her faith, knowing she was going to die. How she could—of all things!—speak of her illness as "God's Christmas present" to her and that her sickness had brought her so close to God.

Carol's roommate, who was a psych major, would have explained away Beth's reactions as "a strong death wish" or as an "understandable psychosomatic reaction" to her illness. But Carol *knew* Beth. She loved her. It just didn't explain how this down-to-earth human being—her *own sister*—could be so sure about her faith, could "accept" life—and death—*knowing* she was going to die.

And then there were Mom and Dad. This was just as hard to understand. She could see them now in the Communion service on Christmas Day. As they looked toward the altar, it seemed there was an invisible bond of—of something, actually connecting them with what was going on at the altar. And something living was coming to them in the words and acts of the pastor and other worshipers in the congregation.

Beth's sickness and death had deeply affected both Mom and Dad. But there was an inner perception—an acceptance—of the same kind Beth had, with which they seemed to give comfort and strength to each other.

It was symbolized in the little touch of love Mom would give Dad when they went to bed at night—since he couldn't hear her with his hearing aid off, she would brush a "good night" across his forehead with her fingers.

And then there were the words of Mom as they walked out to the Mercedes the day she headed back for school.

"Carol, you will find what we have in all of this. God will help you 'understand'—in His own way—if you will just let Him."

And there were the words Dad had said earlier, when he saw her so depressed and confused, sitting alone in her room.

13

"Carol, baby," he had said, "Beth is happy now. And although we all miss her—terribly—you know she wouldn't want you to grieve. She would want you to find the same kind of, well, *peace* that Mom and I have found. But you won't get it brooding here with your own thoughts. It can come only if you let God give it to you through His—well—His *tools* you might call them, there—in your Bible, in rethinking the meaning of your baptism, in letting Him strengthen you in the Lord's Supper."

He stood thoughtfully for a moment, looking out the window. There in the driveway stood the bright red Mercedes, sleek and beautiful and powerful in the radiant sun.

"It's like—well, it's like running that car of yours. I know how much you love it. But it's just a big lifeless piece of tin until you turn the key or feed it some gas and oil." Then he had walked over to Beth's picture and after a moment said quietly, "It's strange how much sorrow we load on our own shoulders because we don't really believe God's promises and make use of the help He wants to give us."

And sitting in class now—the blackboard a little out of focus as she stared beyond it—the prof's words were distant and far away.

In her heart the questions he had raised were still there. They might not be fully answered—at least not in a rational, thoroughly "provable" way. But the bigger question seemed to be what made Beth and Mom and Dad *tick,* what made them come through those tragic days of Christmas vacation—and afterwards—with the calm, the certainty—the same love toward God they had always had. And Mom had said that faith could be hers if she would let God give it to her—in His Word and in the Sacraments.

The bell rang, and Carol made her way out to the parking lot and the Mercedes. The car stood majestically, like a faithful, pedigreed dog waiting for the command of its master.

In one unanticipated motion her hand was on the door handle, and she was in the seat of the car, the door snapping shut firmly behind her with a solid, tight sound. It was quiet inside the car, still and silent. For a moment she sat immobile, fusing herself with the car and its familiar feel.

Then she gave the car life. Her small hand put the key to the ignition, and the Mercedes purred into being, the radio coming on softly. With a finger the steering wheel turned, empowered, the car and the girl as one unit stirring in motion backed out of the parking space.

The car was *her*. It glided straight and true down the lane between rows of parked cars and out onto the main street which led to the dorms on the other side of the campus.

The Listener

The coed sat in the young campus pastor's study. She ran her hands through her short-cropped, curly blonde hair. She was a pretty girl, but her face was lined with anxiety.

The pastor sat quietly at his desk, listening.

"Well, the first problem is with some of the choir members," she began. "As director, there are certain objectives I want to achieve. I'm a music major, you know. And some of the members are there just for the fun of it—or because they're in love with someone in the choir! But they just can't *sing,* Pastor!"

"With that I concur," responded the pastor, chuckling a little.

"And then my other problem is the liturgy. As a new member of the church, it's still a little foreign and strange to me. I'm sure I'll get used to it, but it'll take awhile."

For some time she poured out her feelings. The pastor said little, but as she wound down and began to ask him some pointed questions, he moved into dialog with her. The coed seemed calmer now and after an hour had passed the pastor felt it had been a fairly good counseling session. He had been talking more, and she was sitting there silently. As he finished a long comment on the liturgy, however, something clicked in his brain. It was a statement a prof had made back at the seminary. "Always listen very carefully to the last words a person may say to you as they go out the door. They just might give you a clue as to the real reason they came in to see you."

The pastor stopped talking. The coed said nothing but just stared at a spot on the wall. Biting his tongue, he sought to follow the prof's advice. "*Silence.* Give them *time.*"

A minute went by. The coed crossed her legs and her short skirt inched up her legs. Now the young pastor also found a spot high on the wall and stared at it.

A second minute went by, and a third. *Total silence.* Again the pastor was sorely tempted to say something, *anything,* but he did not open his mouth.

A deep sigh was heard in the room. It came from the coed. Leaning forward she placed her head in both hands and almost choking out the words said, "I guess I should tell you the real reason I came in to see you." She paused. "I've been sleeping with my fiance and just *had* to talk to you about it."

And then the real *counseling began.*

Another hour transpired. And again there was a pause when neither spoke. Off in the distance the campanile tolled the hour.

The coed shifted uncomfortably. "I guess I can't wear my white dress at my wedding now, since you know what I've been doing."

"You certainly can wear your white dress," said the pastor softly. "It may not symbolize your virginity any more, but it *is* a sign of the cleansing forgiveness which you have asked for—and received—through the atoning death of Christ. 'Though your sins are like scarlet, they shall be as *white* as snow.' Through your confession—and commitment to wait with sexual relations until your marriage—and God's response to you through me, your pastor, you have a completely fresh start."

He leaned forward and caught her eyes. "And God doesn't want you to agonize over this any more. Indeed, He's forgotten about it already. For He says, 'I, even I, am He who blots out your transgressions, for My own sake, and remembers your sins no more.' And so you and I need to learn how to pray the little prayer: 'O Lord, forgive me the sin of coming back to You and asking You to forgive a sin You forgave—*and forgot*—a long time ago!'"

Peace came over the coed's face. Again there was silence in the room. But this time it was the silence of peace—and release from the agony of unconfessed and unforgiven sin.

"Would you like to conclude with the Order for Private Confession and Holy Absolution? You know how we discussed it in the adult instruction class when you were coming into the church."

"Oh, yes," the coed responded. And the pastor picked up his stole, put it around his clerical collar, and together they walked out into the sanctuary of the campus chapel.

The coed knelt at the Communion rail and the pastor sat at a prie-dieu near her.

"You have come to make confession before God. In Christ you are free to confess before me, a pastor in His church, the sins of which you are aware and the sins which trouble you."

"I confess before God that I am guilty of many sins. Especially I confess before you that . . ."

"For all this I am sorry and pray for forgiveness. I want to do better . . ."

"Do you believe that the word of forgiveness I speak to you comes from God Himself?"

"Yes, I believe."

"God is merciful and blesses you. By the command of our Lord Jesus Christ, I, a called and ordained servant of the Word, forgive you and your sins in the name of the Father, and of the Son, and of the Holy Spirit."

"Amen."

The coed lifted her head and smiled at the campus pastor. "Thank you," she said simply. The she looked up high in the chancel at the cross. Slowly rising she turned and walked down the center aisle towards the rear of the chapel. Nearing the narthex, she turned and looked at the cross once more. The pastor had said in instruction class that when one receives the Sacrament of Holy Absolution, the Augsburg Confession of the church says it is as if a "voice from heaven" announces, "Your sins are forgiven."

She had heard that voice from heaven. The coed walked out of the chapel and headed for the music building on campus.

For Discussion

A little girl picked up a dust-covered Bible in the living room of her home. "Mommy, whose book is this?" she asked.

"Oh, it's God's book, honey," the mother piously replied.

"Well, then," said the girl, "we'd better send it back to Him, because we're not using it."

1. What do you think was the turning point in Carol's thinking about death and life? *BETH'S SUDDEN DEATH.*
2. What else would you say to Carol if you were her father?
3. In "The Listener," what are the key elements involved in the coed's making a private confession and receiving holy absolution? What are some misunderstandings about this practice? How often should one go? See Matthew 16:19; John 20:23; 2 Corinthians 2:10.
4. How do you evaluate the pastor's handling of the "counseling" situation? See James 1:19.
5. Is it simplistic to say that we don't have more peace and joy because "we just don't use the means of grace"—God's Word and the Sacraments?
6. We can't "renew" our baptismal vow (at confirmation, or daily) because it was totally *God's* work in us. How then do we make it a vital part of our faith-walk every day? See Romans 6:4, 12–13; Ephesians 6:10–18; Philippians 2:12–13.
7. *If one goes to the Lord's Supper every time it is offered it will become more commonplace and less meaningful to a person.* Do you agree?
8. What is your favorite translation of the Bible and why? What beginning steps would you suggest to a new Christian who asks you, "How do I read the Bible?"? *WITH AN OPEN MIND AND WILLINGNESS TO BELIEVE,*

For Further Discussion
Talking about ... Where Is God?
A Transcendent God

9. God is transcendent—above and behind everything. How is this borne out in the following passages? Psalm 10:1; Psalm 139:7–10; Jeremiah 23:23–24; Colossians 1:16–17.

10-1 WHY O LORD DO YOU STAND FAR OFF
18 WHY DO YOU HIDE YOURSELF IN TIMES OF TROUBLE
139-7 WHERE CAN I GO FROM YOUR SPIRIT? WHERE CAN I FLEE FROM YOUR PRESENCES?

An Immanent God

10. But God is also immanent, *present in the world.* He "focused Himself" in a human being. In Jesus Christ, He became Representative Man *for* us. There are always footsteps ahead of you in the Valley of the Shadow, *and they are His.*

    How involved is God in human affairs? our personal lives? The following passages will help you respond: Isaiah 65:24; John 14:27; Acts 2:21; 1 Corinthians 10:13; 1 Thessalonians 5:23–24; Hebrews 4:15.

11. How can you find out who you really are? How does one answer the questions *Who are you? Where are you going?* What is the meaning and purpose of life? In responding, consult these verses: John 8:31–32; Hebrews 10:25; Matthew 22:37; John 15:17.

12. Do I "come to Christ," or does Christ *come to me?* John 15:16; Galatians 2:20; Ephesians 2:8–9.

13. God works through means—His Word and Sacraments. What are the "means of grace," and how does one use them? Acts 17:11; Romans 6:3–4; 1 Corinthians 11:25–29.

"Harry, the vacuum cleaner isn't working again," a woman said to her husband. The man bent over behind the sofa and plugged the cord into the wall.

"You just didn't plug it in, dear," he replied.

Two men spent several hours tearing down the engine of a car, trying to find out why it wouldn't run. Finally, one man said, "Hey, Bill, we're out of gas! *That's* the problem!"

Often we are out of gas. We're out of God. We are not plugged into His Word and Sacraments. But God *does* come to us when we but use His means of grace, the power supply, the channels of His Holy Spirit.

"O taste and see that the Lord is good!" (Psalm 34:8 RSV).

SESSION 2
Happiness

Old Man

The villagers nodded to each other and cast sidelong glances at the familiar figure. "The Old Man is walking again." He was an unkempt old fellow. His disheveled clothes did mean justice to a once-stalwart frame. His bent body always seemed to turn and twist as it followed his restless eyes in constant search and appraisal of his surroundings.

"He's a queer one," a merchant told a customer. "No one seems to know where he came from, or where he lives. He doesn't appear very friendly. But several have told me he's talked to them. Sort of a philosophical old fellow. He gives them advice, they said. Always gives them advice."

The Old Man continued down the street. "He seems to look right through things, I say," a woman plying her broom remarked. "Seems to look at everything as if he knows all about it. And yet he doesn't seem happy. Sort of sad."

On another corner, a Young Man, alive in his youth, stood talking to some companions, their conversation loud, raucous, self-conscious. Their continuous talk was punctuated with loud bursts of laughter. The Young Man listened half-heartedly, somewhat reluctantly, as he stood at the edge of the jesting group. He seemed drawn to the gathering and yet hesitant to share their ribaldry.

Finally, as if in climax, and with noisy, suggestive shouts as to their destination, the young men began to walk up the street, their arms encircled.

At that moment the Old Man appeared and noted the scene. For a brief second his eye caught that of the Young Man. It appeared that some message had passed between them. The Old Man approached the Young Man, oblivious of the others who were calling their companion to join them.

"Good youth," he said, "come hear what an old man has to say." The Young Man paused for a moment, watching his friends walk away. Then, intrigued by the magnetism of the older man's bearing, he followed him. The other young men's shouts died in the distance.

The Old Man and the Young Man walked a short distance and then sat by the side of the road and talked.

"My son," said the Old Man, "beware of evil companions. They are like a snare set in the forest. They appear harmless at first, for you see only the outward leaves of the trees. But outward appearances deceive. A snare captures its victim and that victim is destroyed.

"Evil companions are a snare. They speak as friends. They speak of comradeship. But their deeds are evil and will lead you to ruin and destruction."

The Young Man listened. The Old Man is wise, he told himself. I respect the Old Man's words, he thought.

"Learn now to choose the right path in your youth," the Old Man continued, " . . . for everything in life is emptiness. It is emptiness, pride, and confusion. Listen, I will tell you a story.

"A friend of mine sent me two wreaths of roses. One was genuine, the other was artificial. The friend defied me to detect, without touching, which was false, and which was real. I opened a window and let in a swarm of bees. They at once settled on the genuine roses.

"So you must judge the true values of life. So you must judge your comrades and the pleasures of life. Remember the Giver of your Life and ask Him to show you the abiding values. Guard against the snare in false colors. For so much in life is emptiness—emptiness and pride and confusion."

The Old Man arose and the Young Man watched him walk away and disappear from sight.

The Old Man walked up a great flight of stairs and entered the hall. He cast aside his beggar's rags, and, squaring his shoulders, received the royal robes from his courtier. He crossed the Great Hall and ascended the throne. Leaning forward, his chin in his hand, he gazed nostalgically into space.

"Ah, youth is vanity," he said. He tugged at his dry white beard. "Vanity of vanities, all is vanity."

The court attendants of old King Solomon listened respectfully and, bowing low before their monarch, said:

"Great is Solomon, and long may he live on the earth, O Great and Noble Solomon, O fair and just one, O wise and mighty Solomon."

The Physician

Laughing, Dr. Steven "Skip" Lane pushed open the surgery room door and held it open for his partner, Palmer Evans.

"That's a wrap!" he exclaimed. "Thanks for your help, Palmer."

"You did it," his friend responded. "A brilliant job, as always."

"See you on the golf course!"

"Righto!"

Skip walked down the hall, pulling off his green cap and heading toward the veranda for a breath of air. Ahead of him, outside the intensive care waiting room, stood a small group of people. What an unkempt, scruffy lot, he thought. Their clothes were worn and disheveled, and they huddled together like hobos, totally out of place in the immaculate hospital world. You'd think they'd at least put on clean clothes when they come to a hospital, he mused.

He pushed an elevator button and soon was on the veranda of Alta Bates Hospital, overlooking Berkeley and the Bay Area. He surveyed the scene.

Far out beyond Berkeley he could see The City—San Francisco—and the Golden Gate Bridge, gleaming gold in the morning sun. To his left stretched Oakland. On his right was the University of California—Berkeley, the campanile towering over the campus. Behind him nestled the blue hills, just shaking off the lingering morning fog.

He popped a Coke out of the pop machine and planted his feet squarely. He felt exhilarated. This was *his* world. *Medicine.* And all the fulfillment that came with it.

Only 49 years old, he was already at the top. Besides being considered the best orthopedic specialist in the area, he'd been guest lecturer for a year now at the University of California Medical Center in San Francisco. "You've skipped into the fast lane now, doctor," a friend had complimented him. Skip had smiled wryly at the pun and squared his shoulders in pride.

And he was always cool. Death didn't phase him. He'd been in the Navy Seals. He'd seen some of his buddies drown. Death was part of life. Sooner or later . . . but he was living for *now.* Young doctors phoned him at night for advice. And he's say, "Well now, lad . . . " and share his expertise with them. And he *was* good at his craft. *He* had made it through the rigors of medical school—and totally on his own. He owed *nobody.*

And his physician friends. A great lot! They worked hard, and they worked smoothly together . . . "in sync" they always said. He enjoyed the weekend cocktail parties with the unspoken rule: never discuss politics or religion. And his colleagues clustered around him as he told them the latest joke from the operating room.

Medicine! He loved it. He looked toward the campanile. The Graduate Theological Union was nearby with its several seminaries. He'd thought of going into the ministry once. That was long ago. But he was disenchanted at that time with what he saw in the church—with those people who had little concern for others who were hurting, the sick, or the oppressed. Here at the hospital was *real* "ministry." He laughed at using the word. But in a sense it was correct. This was the true crossroads of life. Sooner or later everyone had to come to a hospital. You certainly couldn't say that about the church. Here was the genuine "temple" of our day. The center of the world. And *he* was at the heart of it!

"Ministry." He let the word roll on his tongue for a moment. A little frown crossed his forehead. Oh, he had to admit that some things seemed to have changed in some churches recently. He recalled some of his friends from college days who'd damned the organized church just as much as he had and had gone into engineering or business. But now, at the age of 35 or even in their 40s, they had gone off for a second career to some seminary. They'd spent four years of their lives, and all their savings, and then taken an appointment to some little parish way out in the boonies. He just couldn't understand it.

Skip walked along the edge of the veranda and looked far out over the bay. A huge aircraft carrier was just coming in under the Golden Gate Bridge. Far to the left a droning 747 lifted off and away from the San Francisco airport. Above the hospital, sea gulls circled in the air like restless kites.

"Ministry." He remembers overhearing two young seminary students in clinical pastoral education chatting at a table near him the other day in the hospital lunch room.

He couldn't recall the exact conversation, but he was struck by their quiet dedication, their concern for the *whole* person, they said, not just being "soul savers." They even spoke of the hospital as their "parish"! And they were grappling with their own faith struggles at the same time. That was clear. But there they were. Emptying bed pans. Going into the clergy. And working with patients like the other hospital staff. A strange new breed!

Skip remembered overhearing one of them praying on the other side of a curtain as he visited a patient in intensive care. It was a simple prayer:

O Lord, we come to You in faith, asking You to relieve the suffering of Your child Patricia. Her life is from You. We know death is not Your will. It comes upon all of us because we are all sinners. Spare Patricia's life, we pray. Forgive us all our sins through the death of Jesus Christ on the cross for us. And when death does come, by Your grace give us what You have sealed to us through our Baptism—eternal life with You, through Jesus Christ our Lord. Amen.

Skip pushed the unrequested memory out of his mind. He turned toward the Berkeley hills and beamed. Just over the hills in Orinda was his home—and Daphne. She would be busy tending her roses now, 34 bushes in all, in their spacious home with pool and spa overlooking the country club.

Daphne! What a woman. She was a practicing Christian, like those sem students were trying to be. She never pushed her religion on him. Thank God. She just quietly said her prayers, read her Bible, attended that little A-frame Lutheran Church on Moraga Way, and ... well ... lived out her faith, I guess you could say.

Skip looked at the hazy blue coastal ridge again. She's just over the hill, he thought. What a woman. They had no children. Daphne couldn't conceive. And they'd always hesitated to adopt a child. But their life was complete otherwise. She was patient with him. Admired him and all he had achieved. She told him he was missing something, but didn't bug him about going to church.

And yet, occasionally she would say, when religion came up, something like, "Skip, you're drinking from a stream the source of which you deny."

His reveries were interrupted by the sound of a familiar voice. Palmer had burst through the veranda door and called Skip's name. Then, seeing him, he had walked slowly toward Skip.

"Brace yourself, old buddy," he said.

"What? ... What is it?" said Skip, baffled by Palmer's unexpected appearance.

"There's been an accident. It's bad news." He paused. "Your wife ... Daphne ... she's dead, Skip. She drowned ... She drowned in your pool."

Skip stood speechless, just staring at Palmer as the whole tragic tale came out. Evidently Daphne had tripped on a rake next to the pool, fallen, hit her head on the diving board, and then dropped into the pool unconscious. A neighbor saw her body when she peered down into the yard from a home on the hill above.

"I've got to go to her!" Skip cried.

But Palmer explained there was nothing he could do. The body was already on the way to the morgue. Friends were at the house. They were stunned. Shocked. Didn't know what to do. They said they would just wait to hear from him.

A long moment of painful silence fell over them. Skip looked up at the hills again. Daphne! How? *Why?*

"What can I do to help, Skip?" Palmer shifted uneasily, not knowing quite what to say. "What can I do?"

"Just leave me alone for a few minutes," Skip said. "I'll be all right."

But he was *not* all right! Anger, disbelief, shock, a scream against God—they all welled up in his throat and just gagged there. But Palmer didn't leave. He just waited quietly on one side of the veranda. Skip stood there staring unseeing up at the hills. His wife was *dead!* Life would never be the same again.

But *what* life? The reality hit him. His whole delicate crystalline existence was shattered.

Finally, Paul slowly walked back to the door. Palmer joined him as they re-entered the hospital.

Two weeks later, the funeral over, Skip finally built up enough strength to go back to work. As he entered the intensive care unit, he saw the same scruffy group of people again. But this time they were standing in a circle, hands joined, evidently saying an intimate prayer together. The scene staggered him. *"My God . . ."* He said it almost as a prayer. Their hearts certainly weren't scruffy. And then he suddenly realized how cruelly he had misjudged them. He felt strangely shamed.

Skip walked, almost staggering now, down the hall. As he turned a corner, he saw the words "Prayer Chapel" on a door. He'd never seen the inside of the room. Hesitating, he opened the door and walked in. It was empty. He sat on a chair and prayed, "Physician, heal thyself."

But he knew he couldn't.

And then he began to remember the one who could.

For Discussion

1. Do you agree?

   The best argument for Christianity is Christians: their joy, their certainty, their completeness. But the strongest argument *against* Christianity is also Christians—when they are somber and joyless, when they are self-righteous and smug in complacent consecration, when they are narrow and repressive, then Christianity dies a thousand deaths. But, though it is just to condemn some Christians for these things, perhaps, after all, it is not just, though very easy, to condemn Christianity itself for them. Indeed, there are impressive indications that the positive quality of joy is in Christianity—and possibly nowhere else. If that were certain, it would be proof of a very high order. (Sheldon Vanusaken, *A Severe Mercy* [San Francisco: Harper and Row, 1980], p. 85.)

2. In "Old Man," doesn't viewing life as vanity lead to a sense of cynicism, hopelessness, and despair?
3. How does one find the balance between a "realistic" view of life and living a "joyful" life? See Proverbs 17:22.
4. An agnostic who had finally joined his wife's church quit in disgust four months later. When asked why, he replied, "They were always so—happy!" What is genuine Christian joy and when is it inauthentic?
5. How does one find true "joy in the Lord"? What was the old man's advice? See John 16:24; Romans 14:17; 1 Corinthians 16:13; Colossians 4:2.
6. In "The Physician," is the description of Dr. Lane's life an implied or unfair generalization about many physicians' lives? Do you think Dr. Lane was really happy?
7. Practically speaking, isn't the hospital more of a "temple" and a "crossroads of culture" than the church? How can or should the church reverse the trend?
8. How do you evaluate Daphne's relationship with her husband?
9. Was Daphne's witness to Skip strong enough? See 1 Peter 3:1–6. What does Scripture mean by "without the word" (v. 1, KJV) or "it will not be necessary for you to say a word" (TEV)? Is explicit *verbal* witness unnecessary? Are people saved by seeing "good examples" of Christianity? How does 1 Peter 3:15–16 relate to the earlier verses in chapter 3 (1–6)?
10. Skip spoke of Daphne as a "practicing Christian." What did he mean?

SESSION 3
Grace/ Thanksgiving

Appreciation

I glanced at my watch as I entered the doctor's office. I was 10 minutes early for my appointment.

As usual. I always worked myself into a lather getting the baby ready to go to the doctor. And then, once I was ready, I didn't want to sit around the house. So here I was, early again.

I looked around the waiting room briefly, then sat down in a chair on the far side of the room. I took the shawl off the baby and straightened my dress a bit.

A man about 40 years old, quite well dressed, sat next to me. He put his magazine aside and smiled at my baby.

"What's her name?" he said in a friendly voice.

"It's a boy," I answered, rather firmly. Then I mellowed a little. "His name is Gary Paul."

"But so much hair!" exclaimed the gentleman.

"Yes, I know," I answered. "When he was born he had more hair than the 29 other babies at the hospital. We like to think he's special."

When I cuddled the baby to me I noted that the man saw the baby's harelip. In the three months since his birth I had gotten used to the inquisitive stares and curious in-

terest of people. But it still pained me to answer their well-meaning questions.

Quickly I began talking in mother-language, looking at the baby: "Yes, little Gary . . . poor little fellow. We love you . . . We'll take good care of you . . ."

"The doctor said they can sew the harelip together when he gets older," I continued. "His isn't as bad as some. When he's fully grown, the doctor said it won't bother him at all."

"It doesn't look bad," the man replied graciously. "You'll never notice it by the time he's a grown man."

I hurried to correct his statement. "Oh, no, the doctor said there would always be a scar. You can always tell when a person has a harelip. I think it's sad a child has to go through life this way. He has only one life, and to have to go through all those years with a blemish like this . . . But he will run and play as other children do. At least he isn't a cripple."

"You should see my boy run," the gentleman said. "He's on the track team in junior high now. Quite a sturdy fellow. He won the 100-yard dash in the county track meet last week. What a boy!

"He's certainly brought a lot of joy to me and my wife. He's a fine specimen of manhood. My wife and I appreciate having such a fine, healthy son."

I'm confident the man didn't mean to make comparisons. But I was touchy about parents who boasted about flawless, healthy children. I had prayed my child would be perfect. And then when he arrived everything had been fine—except the harelip.

The man told me more about his boy—how strong he was, and, again, how much he meant to him and his wife.

Appreciate a healthy boy, I thought. That man doesn't know what it means to appreciate good health. Parents have to experience a heartache as I was having with my son, to understand true appreciation.

The man kept on talking, with a warm light in his eyes as he spoke with pride about his son.

Resentfully, I finally terminated the conversation and began to fuss with the baby's clothes.

Suddenly the reception door opened.

A woman entered carrying a small young boy on her arm. I sensed something was wrong with the child. When the woman turned, I saw his face. The eyes were white and sightless. And the little head rolled around loosely, without control.

Together with the occupants of the waiting room I felt that strange embarrassment one always shares with the parents of an abnormal child. The mother shifted the helpless child on her arm, avoiding the eyes of people in the room.

When the woman saw the man in the chair next to me, she walked over and began speaking to him.

"Sorry I'm late, dear," she said. "I had to wait for a taxi to come down here. Sure glad you could get off work."

"I'll take him, honey." The man took the helpless child into his arms, and fondled him affectionately. "There, there, Jimmy," he said. Though the child was blind, he responded with a smile.

I looked at the man wonderingly. Hardly knowing what to say, I asked, "He's your boy? But I thought your boy was in junior high."

"Yes, that's our other boy," the gentleman replied. "We're really proud of him. Makes one appreciate the blessings God gives a person who has a fully developed, healthy child.

"But we are proud of our Jimmy, too. And we're going to do everything we can for him, aren't we, Jimmy?" He hugged the little boy and clasped him to his shoulder.

Suddenly I found a great deal of rearranging to do with my baby's clothes. I flushed as a guilty sense of shame swept over me.

I looked at my child. He smiled at me, beautifully. I pressed him to my breast and took a long, deep breath.

Dear God, I prayed, forgive me for not being thankful for what I have. Help me appreciate my blessings.

Hello, Jan

She was on the plane to see her mother, and then . . .
"Hello, Jan."

"Well, hello. Who are you?"

The minute Jan said the words she knew who it was and where she was. She did not feel fear, and yet she was puzzled as the face stared at her. It was a most unusual face—at once stern and yet full of compassion.

She blinked. "How did I get here?" she asked.

"It was a plane crash," the voice answered. "You were on your way to visit your mother."

"Oh," Jan sighed.

"How has it been going, Jan?" the voice said.

"What do you mean?" she responded. And then her usual spunk came quickly to the surface. "I think I've been doing quite well. Look, I've tried to be as faithful a Christian as I know how. I really mean that. And not—and not just going through the motions, either. I love the Lord, my family, the work I do. Look how I've given myself for my kids. I love my church. I pray. I work hard in all that I do. I think I've been doing all right."

The voice was gentle, yet quite firm. "But at times, Jan, you have been testing God's grace. You have been taking God's patience a little too lightly."

"What do you mean?" Jan said. Immediately she knew the answer she was going to hear. There were no secrets now—not in this place.

"You were a faithful Christian," the voice responded. "You served the Lord well, and for many years. We up here know about that. And others saw Christ in you. But recently you have been taking your faith and your salvation too much for granted. You—"

Suddenly Jan's composure broke and she cried out, "But I gave my whole life to God! I love the Lord! I *enjoy* going to church. I want to be a good Christian. I've worked hard to be faithful to Christ. It's been a long, hard life. I think I deserve . . . "

She stopped, then paused and looked sideways, hesitating, then down at the floor.

"Deserve," said the voice gently. "That was the problem. You believed you were saved by grace—by the free gift of God's love in Christ's dying for you on the cross. And that's true. But lately you had begun to act and live as if you were paying God back, as it were with your 'faithful Christian life.'

"Sure, you were an exemplary Christian. But it was getting to be 'cheap grace' for you. Every morning you would get up and pray—oh, sure, we heard you—but each day wasn't much different than the last. You went through the same patterns, the same rationalizations, then the same plea for forgiveness. God is patient just so long. And what you sow, you reap. Simple equation, isn't it?

"There have been times you felt very thankful to God. And you have been blessed a great deal—right? But you still didn't share as much as you could with others around you who were hurting, who were without jobs, who were hungry."

Jan straightened up, and with a feeling of resignation said, "What do I do now?"

"Well, what do you have to say for yourself?" said the voice.

The silence was deafening.

"I have nothing to say for myself," she replied. "Lord Jesus Christ, help me . . . "

Suddenly everything was changed. Jan paused a moment and then said, "What just happened? How did I get in *here?*"

"Just receive it," said the voice. "It's a gift. If you really give Our Lord the total credit for your being here . . . all is well . . . "

"This is fantastic," Jan cried. "I just wish I could go back and tell others about this, my family, my friends . . . "

"But they have the Scriptures, the church, their fellow Christians," said the voice. "They have been warned . . . and promised God's grace. Just so long as it is not misused—taken for granted."

The voice paused. "There's someone here who has been waiting to see you."

Jan took a deep breath. "You mean . . . ?"

"Yes," the voice said. For a moment, Jan hesitated.

"There is no reason to be afraid," the new voice said.

The airplane's wheels bumped once, then twice as the aircraft made a choppy landing. Jan's eyes opened, startled, and she sat bolt upright in her seat.

Outside she could see her mother at the terminal gate waiting for her.

"Oh, Mother! God!" she cried silently to herself.

"I *will* change. I *will* be different . . . each day. I *do* thank You, Lord, for your patience with me. Help me not to take Your grace and forgiveness so lightly."

And far in the back of her mind she could hear a small, quiet voice saying, "We'll see . . . "

For Discussion

The life which is lived in response to grace is also the life which is thankful (Earl Gaulke).

Here are the words of a young mother, Phyllis Kester, who barely escaped death with her two boys and her husband in an auto accident. He was completely encased in the car from his neck down, with just a few inches of clearance all around his head. A truck doing 75 mph hit them head on, killing the driver.

She wrote:

> So we are all back together in Baytown for Christmas and are very thankful. The Scripture Ephesians 5:20—"Giving thanks always for all things unto God and the Father in the name of our Lord Jesus Christ"—really had an impact on me the night of the accident after we got to a hospital. During one of Monty's brief conscious moments I told him that the boys and I were fine, and he immediately responded by thanking and praising God. It really spoke to my heart to see him lying there in all his pain and still able to thank God for the situation. Nearly all Monty's cuts have healed completely now, and he will have only very minor scars on his face. His ear seems to be healing, so he'll keep his hearing and the surgery that put a pin in his left leg just below his hip is doing fine. He is up and about on crutches now and doesn't even look as if he was in a wreck. This whole experience has really shown us how true Philippians 4:19 is: "But my God shall supply all your need according to His riches in glory by Christ Jesus." The Lord really has

provided our every need in everything, even down to the tiny details. I wish I could somehow express the joy and peace we feel for having gone through this experience and all it has taught us.

1. Can one really "thank" God for trials and suffering? See James 1:2 ff.; 1 Peter 2:20; Philippians 4:4; 1 Thessalonians 5:18.
2. A pastor said he always has two lists of the people in his congregation. One is the list of the people who are sick, and he's praying they'll get well. The other is a list of people who are well, and he's praying they'll get sick.

   "The knees of some people are so stiff that sometimes God has to knock their owners down before they'll make use of them."

   Can a Christian *really* say "Why *not* me, Lord?" rather than "Why *me,* Lord?" Should a Christian *ask* for suffering? Isn't that masochistic? See Hebrews 12:5–8.
3. If Scripture says in tribulation we are to "share in Christ's sufferings" (1 Peter 4:13), does that mean we participate in some meritorious way in His suffering and death for us? See Ephesians 2:8–10.
4. How does one bear up under suffering? See 1 Corinthians 10:13. Just what *is* the "way of escape"?
5. In what priority would you list things in a prayer of thanksgiving to God? See: 1 Corinthians 15:57; Deuteronomy 8:10; Psalm 100:4; Colossians 1:12; 3:15.
6. "How does one get forgiveness from God?" the Sunday school teacher asked her class. There was no answer. In exasperation the teacher asked the question again, "How does one get forgiveness from God?" Finally a boy in the back row raised his hand and said, "Sin!"

   Thinking of Jan on the airplane, what is the difference between "cheap grace" and "costly grace"? See Matthew 16:24; 21:30; Luke 14:26–27, 33; Galatians 5:24; Philippians 3:8; 1 Peter 2:21.

   (See also Dietrich Bonhoeffer, *The Cost of Discipleship* [New York: Macmillan, 1959], 35–38. Also, see David P. Scaer, "Sanctification in Lutheran Theology," *Concordia Theological Quarterly* 49 [April–July, 1985]: 181.)

7. Martin Luther said *"Pecca fortiter!"* ("Sin boldly.") St. Augustine said "Love God—and do as you please." Dietrich Bonhoeffer said "Now [one] can be a sinner and still enjoy the grace of God" (*Life Together* [San Francisco: Harper and Row, 1954], 113.)

   Isn't one actually a fatalist—or a hypocrite—if you know you're going to sin anew each day, and then ask God's forgiveness every night?

8. Does "being saved by grace" mean we don't do *anything* about our life-in-God? Are we just lifeless garden hoses through which God's grace flows? See Matthew 5:16; 1 Timothy 6:18; Titus 2:7; James 2:17–18; 1 Peter 2:12.

9. Gratitude in our everyday language means to pay someone back: "Out of gratitude for you having us over to your house for dinner, we are going to invite you to our home." Isn't it wrong then to speak of having "gratitude" toward God? Can we "pay Him back"? See Ephesians 2:8–9; Philippians 2:12–13.

SESSION 4
Loneliness

The Visit

Old Bill Perkins had been waiting for three days now for his son to come by. Young Bill had phoned him Sunday afternoon and said he'd be in the area on his sales calls. They set up a luncheon date for this Wednesday noon. *Today!*

Old Bill, 85, still lived alone. He managed quite well, he assured himself. Though Emily had been dead for 20 years, he still missed her a lot. But he had his friends, his church. And his ample Navy pension took care of his needs.

He lived in a little cottage behind a three-story apartment building in Berkeley. There were always students around. Young life! Bill loved watching them. They were *so young,* so eager. They appeared younger every year. Though they felt mature, they had much to learn. So much ahead of them.

Bill had risen early, as always, and had a light breakfast. Fully dressed, sporting his favorite necktie and sports jacket, he waited eagerly for his son.

He walked out of the cottage door and checked his tomatoes. How proud he was of them!

Across the back fence he saw his neighbor, Harry Talmadge, who immediately called out to him, "Well, Bill, you are really spiffed up today! What's the occasion?"

"My son! It's my son, Bill! He's coming for lunch today," he grinned. The two men chatted amiably until Harry's wife called him from the back door.

Old Bill looked around his little domain for a moment. He had much to be thankful for. When he rose, he had swung his legs out of the bed, crossed himself, and said, "Good morning, Lord! Thank You for another day! I praise You, Lord!"

Old Bill felt most grateful because he didn't need to live in a rest home as some of his friends whom he visited regularly did. It was so sad to see some of them going downhill. There were those who talked to themselves all day. Others rode up and down in the elevator, endlessly. Some straightened chairs and rearranged newspapers. Others sat alone in their rooms, rocking, waiting for the relatives who never appeared.

Old Bill shook his head, and broke out into a grin again. His roses were doing beautifully, too.

Beyond another fence he saw Mrs. Garner peer from behind a cautiously drawn curtain. On the sauce most of the time, she would be bombed out of her gourd in as little as two hours. He wished he could help her.

But Bill was coming! He would tell him about some of his war experiences again. He really had had them! *Two* wars! And all the funny things that had happened to him! He couldn't wait to tell those stories again.

The morning hours dragged by, but at 11:30 young Bill, dressed in a gaudy jacket, appeared. Or rather, "Big Bill" Perkins. The elder Bill was extremely proud of him. A salesman, he had much of the old salt in him! Bill immediately gave Old Bill a big hug. He's a genuine back-slapper, Old Bill thought happily as he returned the hug.

"Glad to see you again, Son! It's been a while . . . "

"Can't stay as long as I thought, Dad. I have an early appointment, but I'm here," young Bill responded.

Old Bill looked at his son sideways as they entered the cottage and headed for the tiny breakfast nook. His heart sank at hearing his son's words. But he didn't want to criticize. Be thankful he's here, he told himself. He never got to see much of him, but he didn't want to intrude or be a nuisance. And he was proud of his son.

"I've made something special for you for lunch," he quipped cheerily. "It's my own vichyssoise. I serve it cold. You'll really like it!"

"I'd really prefer hot soup, Dad."

"Oh, just wait. You'll see!"

As young Bill seated himself at the tiny dinette table the doorbell rang.

Old Bill, startled, turned to his son. "Wonder who could that be?" He hurried to the door and opened it.

"Well, Pastor Schmidt! So good to see you! Come on in! This is an unexpected surprise!"

Old Bill ushered the young pastor into the cottage, and, smiling broadly, began a little jig. The gold in his teeth took on new luster. "I've got *two* visitors now!" he exclaimed as he swirled and bounced around the tiny kitchen chuckling to himself.

"Sit down, pastor," he bubbled. "Join us for lunch. It'll only be a moment. You remember my son, Bill."

Ignoring "Big Bill" Perkins' stare from across the table, Pastor Homer Schmidt blurted, "Mr. Perkins, would you like to have Holy Communion?"

Old Bill looked quizzically at the young man. "But I'm not dying, Pastor! I'll be in church next Sunday. Here, have some of my special vichyssoise!"

The three sat down, after Old Bill led them in a brief prayer. The two younger men looked at each other with raised eyebrows as they put spoonfuls of the cold soup into their mouths. Bill talked about his tomatoes, his roses, and the young people in the nearby apartment building, as the other two listened in silence.

Then he suddenly jumped up from the table and sailed into some of his "war stories." A few moments later, noting the passiveness of the two younger men, Old Bill quickly said, "Pastor, I don't think I've done my 'Popeye' dance for you! Look at this!" he chortled, with a twinkle in his eye. Then Old Bill danced a jig around the little table, ending with a "poop-poop" whistle which made the younger men laugh.

For just a split second, Old Bill wondered if they had been laughing *with* him or *at* him. But he didn't have time to decide, for suddenly his son was on his feet. "Sorry, Dad, I have to go. My appointment, you know."

Young Pastor Homer Schmidt decided to leave, too. He had an appointment at church.

"I'll see you again soon, Dad," young Bill said as they walked toward the door.

I wonder, Old Bill thought to himself. *Even though you live nearby, I see you less now than when you lived a thousand miles away a few years ago.*

Their good-byes quickly exchanged, Old Bill stood at the cottage door as the two younger men walked away from him, down the driveway towards their cars.

Bill stood with his head erect, looking dignified in his favorite jacket and tie. But then his face changed. He was not crying, but the sides of his cheeks started jerking in a near sob. Tears began to appear in his eyes, and on his face was a look into the yesterdays of long-gone joys and the tomorrows of more emptiness.

Old Bill watched their forms retreating farther down the driveway.

"They could have stayed just a little bit longer," he sighed.

He walked slowly back into the cottage, and sat down in the living room in front of the TV set. He did not turn it on. He just sat and stared at the lifeless screen.

That is the story of my life now, he mused.

A blank screen.

He sighed again.

Then he blinked back some more tears and looked up high and far left into a meaningless spot in space.

His lips and jowels quivered uncontrollably, but he resisted the temptation to sob.

Now talking to himself, he said, "They could have stayed just a little bit longer."

Maybe he *should* have told his son about the verdict the doctor had given him after his last physical examination on Monday.

But he didn't want to worry young Bill. *"Big* Bill."

He was doing so well in business. There would be plenty of time to tell him.

Time. He had plenty of it. No. He didn't, he corrected himself. The doctor had said it would be soon, though not painful. *He* could prepare *himself* for the end. He had done so many things alone since Emily died. He could take care of himself . . . .

No. *He* wouldn't take care of himself.
Christ would.
But they could have stayed just a little bit longer.

The Widow

Marian glanced at the couples assembled at Ethel and Jim's party.

Couples! That was the "state of the art." As it always had been! Widows didn't fit in.

Oh, her friends had reached out to her after her husband, Bill, had drowned in a boating accident on Mille Lacs Lake. They brought in food after the funeral. They stayed to visit. Conversation was difficult, however. They appeared *embarrassed* by Bill's death. They didn't know what to say.

"Marian!" a friend, Jane, bubbled. "So good to see you again!" Marian's thoughts jerked back to the present, and she smiled back.

"Come join me and Ed at our table." Seating herself, Marian listened to conversation about the kids. After a few moments she felt Ethel tap her shoulder.

"Oh, Marian, I hate to disturb you. Would you mind, we have this new couple on the block and I *so* did want Ed and Wilma to meet them. Would you mind sitting somewhere else?"

"Not at all," Marian answered graciously. I don't mind at all." (*Liar!* she chided herself.)

Marian moved to the Johnsons' table, where she was warmly received. She noted one empty chair. They chatted amiably for a while. But just as Marian reached for her tomato juice, Ethel returned.

"Marian, you *dear!* Do you mind? I promised the Haggertys they could sit with these people. They're bridge partners, you know. You're a *dear!*"

Marian rose and walked to the side of the room again. She stood there for a few moments, alone. This time she could really tell that peoples' darting eyes were trying to avoid her.

Of course. She was looking at "the couples' world."

At that moment, her brother Jack arrived. He caught the look in her eyes, and said, "Marian! Come over here and join us. It's a big table. We'll make room for you."

That's the way that evening passed.

And many more.

Marian Adams. Widow. Fifty-five. Blond—no gray hair. Still attractive, often stunning. But *alone*.

No children during 30 years of marriage. God knows how they had wanted them.

And God knows how much she had loved Bill. And theirs had been such a full, blessed, and happy union.

But then the unexpected had happened. Just when Bill, a mechanic, had finally gotten his own shop behind their home in Willmar, there was *the accident*.

He had been out on the lake alone, going for northerns. An experienced fisherman, he always wore a life-jacket. But according to local residents, the sudden squall had been the worst in 50 years. Bill's boat had capsized and the waves had finally overcome him. They found his floating body, hours later, far from shore.

Never again would he come back to his beloved shop behind the house where he worked on cars all day. Never again would he step the few feet to the back door and yell jauntily to her, "Hi, honey, I'm home for lunch!"

Never again would he and Marian walk the 10 blocks to the Willmar Lutheran Church. Or in midwinter stop halfway at the well-heated small Episcopal Church to warm their half-frozen hands and feet at the old stove in the center of the nave.

Never again.

Oh, how Bill had loved fishing and hunting with his friends. But that was all over now. His name was no longer on the bank statement or the church rolls. Occasionally Marian imagined she saw him in a crowd on the street. She'd rush forward and begin to cry out to him. But the figure would turn to reveal a stranger. She no longer dreamed about Bill. He didn't *exist*. He was *dead*.

And she was a widow. *Alone*.

One day Marian sat in her mother's old easy chair in the quiet of her living room. It was the chair she had died in.

She looked at Bill's prize catch hanging over the fireplace mantel—a 30-pound stuffed northern pike. For many years he had bragged about that one to his friends.

Suddenly the doorbell rang. That's unusual, Marian mused. People don't call on me anymore. After several months she'd overheard them say, "Oh, she's doing *so* well now! She's got it together. I'm so proud of her!"

They didn't know. But it was *then* that the grief had taken over.

Marian opened the front door.

Harriet. In her wheelchair. Smiling radiantly up at Marian, she chirped, "Hi, you old turkey! I've missed you. So I thought I'd drop by. I've just returned from the Mayo Clinic in Rochester. Thought I'd say hi."

Delighted, Marian pushed the front door open and helped Harriet get her wheelchair over the doorsill.

When they had settled themselves in the living room, Harriet turned to Marian.

"They've forgotten you, haven't they?"

Startled, Marian asked, "Who?"

"Your friends," Harriet answered.

"Well, not really," Marian responded. "I've been invited out a lot. But more recently, well, I just didn't care to go. I—"

"I know," Harriet said quietly. "I've been there."

Silence, their trusted friend, settled around them.

"Let me tell it like it is," she said, slapping the right arm of her wheelchair.

"Our answer is from Betty Elliot. You know—the famous Christian author we saw interviewed on TV, remember? She talked about her solution—well, not *solution,* but *experience*—with loneliness. Or I should say *coping* with it and discovering the blessing of solitude.

"You know, Marian, loneliness doesn't have to be a pit. It can be a well." She laughed, "As Henri Houwen says, a personal well which can become 'an inexhaustible source of beauty and self-understanding.'"

Marian rested her head on the back of her mother's chair. Not stiffly, but relaxed. Harriet was a friend. A true friend.

She could trust her. She could be herself with her. All defenses down. Harriet knew suffering. And pain. Though she hadn't courted it, she accepted it. She was one of the few she'd met who didn't say "Why me, Lord?" but "Why *not* me, Lord?"

She was willing to partake in Christ's suffering. And she called it an *honor* to serve that way!

What a grace-filled woman! Marian thought. What a dear, dear friend.

You don't "*make* friends." They are a gift of God.

Harriet continued. "Remember, Betty Elliot lost two husbands. One, a missionary killed in Ecuador. The other died of cancer. So she's been there, too.

"Be still and know that God is God. Give thanks to Him for the promise of His presence. He's still in charge. And He's preparing a place *for us*—and preparing *us for*—the wonderful things to come."

"I believe that with all my heart," Marian answered quietly, looking lovingly at her friend sitting in front of her in her wheelchair.

"This next advice is tougher," Harriet told Marian.

"Refuse self-pity! That's a death that has no self-resurrection. Don't mope over loving Bill—or envy your friends who still have their husbands."

Harriet paused a moment, then said softly, "Christ bore and carried our sorrows—not that we might not suffer, but that our suffering might be like His.

"'To hell, then, with self-pity!'

"Pardon my French!" Harriet chuckled again.

Marian sat inert, drinking in all Harriet was saying. She knew Harriet wasn't just quoting Betty Elliot. She *believed* what she was saying.

She incarnated it.

"Accept your loneliness. It can be a stage—a vocation—to realize your helplessness—and be drawn closer to God."

"*Accept* it?" cried Marian. "That's awfully hard, Harriet. I don't know if I can."

"*Offer up your loneliness to God.* Give it to Him as a gift and let Him transform it."

"But how?" Marian asked.

"Numero lasto!" Harriet interrupted. "Do something for someone else. Plan each day . . . some specific thing . . . not to satisfy yourself but to meet the needs of others."

Harriet sighed softly and looked deeply into the eyes of her dear old friend. Again came the long, trusted silence.

"*Pour yourself out,* Marian," she said.

Harriet paused for a moment and then threw her head back. "Well, so there's my little 'sermon' for the day!"

"Harriet, that's no sermon," Marian replied. "That really makes sense to me—God's sense. I only hope I have the grace to live it out."

They chatted for some time.

But finally Harriet slumped forward in her wheelchair.

"Harriet, are you all right?" Marian said, rising to her feet.

"Of course. Time for my pills. Just help me out the front door and I can be down the block and home in five minutes."

"But can't I go with you?"

"No need. Self-dependency, you know! Very important! My niece, Brita, is home. She'll help me. I don't want to be treated like a cripple!"

Marian helped Harriet out the front door, remembering it was time for her pills, too.

She bolted the front door and returned to the living room. Bill's fish over the fireplace. Her mother's old chair. The corner of the room where they'd always placed their little Christmas tree.

She walked through the dining room and into the kitchen. Through the window, beyond her little potted plants, she saw the old garage where Bill had worked so long and lovingly on his friends' cars.

Dear Bill. Dear Harriet. Dear God.

I love you all. Even my well-meaning, forgetful friends.

She walked into her bedroom and unscrewed the cap of the bottle with her heart pills. She swallowed them slowly—with water. Then she drew the blinds and pulled down the blanket of her bed and lay down.

It had been an exhilarating hour with Harriet. She needed to calm down. Harriet's ideas on coping with loneliness were helpful and certainly practical. If she just had the patience to put them into practice.

Slowly she closed her eyes. And soon she began to dream. Of Bill! She saw him approach her.

"We'll be together again," he said. She sensed her body, like a shadow, rise up from her still form on the bed and move toward her husband.

In her dream she saw Bill reach out his hand to greet her.

But it was not a dream.

For Discussion

1. Who are widows and widowers in your congregation? (Why not actually list them?) Who is ministering to their needs? What are their specific needs? See Acts 6:1–6; 1 Timothy 5:3, 8.
2. How would you expand on each of the six points Elizabeth Elliot makes? What would you add?

    1. "Be still and know that God is God" (Psalm 46). Set aside a definite time for Bible reading and prayer.
    2. Give thanks—for the promise of God's presence. He's still in charge—and is preparing "for us" an eternal weight of glory beyond all comparison.
    3. Refuse self-pity—a death that has no resurrection. Don't dwell on your own losses—or envy others. Christ bore and carried our sorrow—not that we might not suffer, but that our suffering might be like His.
    4. Accept your loneliness. It can be a stage—a vocation— to realize our helplessness and be drawn closer to God.

5. Offer up your loneliness to God . . . Give it to Him as a gift and let Him transform it.
6. Do something for somebody else. Take definite, overt action to overcome the inertia of grief. (See Isaiah 58:10–12) Pour yourself out.

(Adapted from Elisabeth Elliot, "The Ones Who Are Left," *Christianity Today,* Feb. 27, 1976, p. 7)

God says: "I know your depression. I care for you." "I will never leave you, nor forsake you" (Hebrews 13:5 NKJV).
3. What widow or widower do you know who has risen above loneliness? What is the key to that person's life?
4. What is meant by "trusted silence" in the story?
5. What guidelines should be followed in visits to those mature in years? (Mature = "seeking wisdom.")
6. Besides the elderly who may be lonely, what other persons in your congregation, regardless of age, may be suffering from loneliness? How are you reaching out to them?
7. What is the difference between loneliness and solitude?

There was a woman, a happy and efficient wife of a pastor, who was experiencing her full share of life's sunshine and shade, but no real darkness falling her way. And then, suddenly, without warning, her husband died of a heart attack, leaving her terribly alone and afraid; afraid of her own decisions, afraid of the present, afraid of the future. When a pastor visited her, he related how she was in the viselike grip of fear—so tyrannized that most of her time was spent in bed. She was so terrified that she became bedridden.

When the minister saw her two years later, he was pleasantly surprised to find a poised, serene woman, working as a receptionist in an insurance office. When the pastor asked her to explain her amazing recovery, the woman replied, "The work helped, of course, but I couldn't work at all until I faced my fear and saw it was basically a selfish rebellion against God and what I thought was 'God's will.' When I saw that, I began to pray that God would forgive my selfishness. And as I prayed, I became aware of God's hand reaching down to me, and the Holy Spirit moved me to reach up in faith until I finally clasped that hand. And then to my amazement, I found His hand clasping mine, and I knew that He really cared and that He would help me as long as I held His hand in faith."

What was the clue to the change in that woman's life? See Psalm 68:6, 139:7–10; Isaiah 41:10, 43:1, 49:16, 65:24; John 16:33; Hebrews 1:14.

SESSION 5
Aging

The Memory

Bishop Winston Arthur Attenborough II squared his shoulders and looked at the long line of clergy assembled ahead of him outside St. Alban's Cathedral in Richmond, Virginia. Their gowns billowed in the warm September sunshine as the last worshipers moved toward the church narthex.

The cathedral tower bell tolled deeply every 10 seconds. It tolled for his friend, Canon Paul Evans. Two weeks before, Paul had died of a heart attack at age 60. He had been buried down in South Carolina where he and his wife, Charlotte, had taken an early retirement because of his ill health. And a memorial service in his honor was being held today at the cathedral where he had been on the staff for 10 years.

Winston asked another clergyman to hold his bishop's crook, while he adjusted the uncomfortable miter on his head.

Sixty-two years old, square-jawed, six feet six inches tall, he stood well above his fellow clergy.

He wondered how many services, dedications, ordinations, installations of priests he had attended since becoming bishop eight years ago. Sylvia, his wife, had always accompanied him. Then three years ago she died suddenly as a result of a car accident. Her car had skidded on ice on the north Richmond freeway and had hit a bridge abutment.

Dear Sylvia! Though he missed her dreadfully, he had adjusted to a single life. But then there was Charlotte . . .

When the Dean of the cathedral beckoned to Winston, he stepped through the assembled clergy to the rear of the nave of the church. Balancing his bishop's crook squarely on the red-carpeted center aisle, Winston surveyed the packed cathedral. He looked down the long aisle to the cross gleaming in the afternoon sun on the high altar. Above, on each side, were the treasured windows, their blue leaded glass reminiscent of the famous, age-old blue windows at the Chartres Cathedral in France.

The mighty chords of the organ suddenly stopped. Silence filled the great building. A young clergyman stepped forward and held the service book open for Winston.

In a booming voice, Winston called out, "Blessed be the God and Father of our Lord Jesus Christ, the Father of mercies and God of all comfort, who comforteth us in all our affliction, that we may be able to comfort them that are in any affliction, through the comfort wherewith we ourselves are comforted of God!"

At the first sound of Winston's voice, a number of heads jerked, startled, as they heard his stentorian words ring through the cathedral.

His voice continued, mesmerizing the worshipers as they sat rigid in the pews, facing the altar.

"I would not have you to be ignorant, concerning them which are asleep, that ye sorrow not, even as others which have no hope. For if we believe that Jesus died and rose again, even so them also which sleep in Jesus will God bring with Him."

The clergy in the narthex now began to move slowly past the bishop, as Winston intoned the third verse:

"I know that my Redeemer liveth, and that He shall stand at the latter day upon the earth. And though after my skin worms destroy this body, yet in my flesh shall I see God; whom I shall see for myself, and mine eyes shall behold, and not another."

The clergy moved past Winston now, down the long center aisle. He handed the book back to the priest and took his place at the end of the procession.

The organist introduced an Easter hymn, and, as one person, the huge congregation rose to their feet and sang:

Alleluia! Alleluia! Alleluia!
The strife is o'er, the battle done;
Now is the Victor's triumph won;
Now be the song of praise begun. Alleluia!

Winston raised his head in elation as the stirring singing engulfed him. Ahead of him he saw the dignified clergy, swaying back and forth in procession. How many now had white or graying hair, he thought. It seemed such a short time since their hair had been black or blonde. His bishop's miter covered his bald head!

Aging, he thought. I don't feel like I'm 62. I feel I'm 34, or 42, or 55. But not 62! I wonder what it would be like to be born old, and grow young! What an idea! But how would it stop? He remembered what one physician had told a mother who had just given birth to a child, "Make sure you like what you have, because we'd have a heck of a time putting it back!"

He was suddenly jolted back to the present when he saw Charlotte. There she was, sitting in the front row between her two grown sons, Peter and Jeffrey.

Charlotte! With what dignity she carried herself! Her slightly graying hair was upswept now, tucked under a striking white, broad-rimmed hat. Only Charlotte could get away with wearing such a hat to her husband's funeral! Her features were sharp, her nose aquiline, her head held high.

Charlotte!

Memory pulled him back 25 years into the past. But it wasn't "past." It was now. *Today.* This very moment.

Memory is not the past. It is contemporary, he mused. It is the context of what I think and do *today.*

A sudden memory of his wife, Sylvia, and their only child, Alexia, flashed through his mind. Alexia had died of leukemia two weeks following the doctor's diagnosis, after winning the Miss Teen Virginia talent award, some 20 years ago. He could still visualize the final night of the pageant, when she became the first of three finalists. Poised, confident, striking, she had walked out on the stage, in her full-length green gown, to the thunderous applause of her fellow-contestants and hundreds of parents. She had played a version of "Malaguena" in just two minutes. And then finally, she had been named the first-place winner!

But she was gone. With the Lord—and now, so was Sylvia. He was here, alone, walking down the aisle. At his friend, Paul's, memorial service. And Charlotte, Paul's widow, was there ahead of him in the front pew.

Bishop Winston Attenborough entered the chancel and seated himself in the bishop's chair. Long banks of stalls on either side of the chancel were filled with clergy. Ahead of them were prayer desks, each with a tiny yellow lamp-shade, as in St. Paul's, London; and below them were the choir boys, neatly dressed in gray suits and large white collars.

The Scripture readings began. Winston looked at Charlotte again, and she stared clearly, steadily, back at him.

Memory! He recalled the time 30 years ago when he had first met her at a cocktail party for the local clergy. He was a young priest then, married to Sylvia only a few years.

But Charlotte had intrigued him. They had talked together over their drinks, and, quite simply, had fallen in love.

He recalled they had walked out behind their friend's huge Southern manse for a while. They conversed under a massive Magnolia tree, very much drawn to each other.

He had been tempted to kiss her, he recalled, and that had scared him. Soon, however, they were back in the house again, and separated—until the next morning, when he dropped by her home, knowing her husband was at the rectory preparing his sermon.

Then they had *really* talked. Long and intensely, over her freshly ground Colombian coffee.

But then, it was over. The dream remained, but life went on as before. They saw each other occasionally at diocesan conferences or parties, but they never phoned or tried to meet each other. It was only that cliche'd-but-true "look across a crowded room."

Again Winston was jolted back to the present by the choir's moving rendition of his favorite "O Jesu, Grant Me Hope, and Comfort." How often he had sung that himself during the Advent season, in the choir back home in Hampstead, Massachusetts!

55

And now the sermon. Glancing at his watch, Winston settled his big frame into the ill-fitting wooden stall. Please, Harold, no more than 10 minutes! he prayed.

Harold Mitchell. They would ask *him* to be the preacher! But then he had been Paul's closest staff associate at the cathedral.

"Paul was a faithful priest," Harold began, after he'd read the text and addressed a few personal words to Charlotte and her family. "He loved the Lord, and he gave of himself totally in his ministry to other people."

True, thought Winston. Too bad he was such a negativist, cynicist, and super-conservative theologian!

Sorry, Lord, he apologized, glancing up at the ceiling of the high-arched chancel. Just remembering . . ..

"Paul cared for his congregation above everything else . . ." Harold continued.

That's true, Winston sighed. And he also ran his early parishes by intimidating people, and the utilization of administration-by-crony—*his* cronies. Paul thought he had charisma, kissing the ladies all the time, and praising the men—if they did things *his* way.

Sorry, Lord! Winston groaned again, and looked heavenward. I must admit Paul mellowed when he came to the cathedral. He learned to work with a team. And his illnesses gave him keener perspectives. Poor Charlotte! Dear, dear Charlotte. What all she'd gone through over the years.

Paul was frail, as we all are. The church is so *human,* Winston thought. We are *all* so human. Why don't the critics of the church make a distinction between Christ and His followers? Between the church as the body of Christ and the church as an organization full of weak people?

And yet, those outside the church want to see Christianity in action. What is "Christianity" without authentic Christians *living out* their Christian walk in the world?

Harold had finished his sermon now, and the congregation rose to sing a hymn Winston had suggested be sung at his own funeral:

Lord, Thee I love with all my heart;
I pray Thee, ne'er from me depart.
With tender mercy cheer me.
Earth has no pleasure I would share,

*Yea, heav'n itself were void and bare
If Thou, Lord, wert not near me.*

The organ swelled again, and the choir boys came in with a soaring descant high above the other singing—like a legion of visiting angels:

*Lord Jesus Christ, my God and Lord, my God and
   Lord
Forsake me not! I trust Thy Word!*

Winston glanced toward Charlotte. She stood in the front row, erect, her head held high. Their eyes met. She knew her husband for what he had been and had not been. She had loved him. But many years before, she had told Winston that she loved him, too. And he had loved Sylvia, and Charlotte, too.

They just were different kinds of love.

The organist improvised for a moment, lifting the entire congregation to an even higher pitch, and then they all exulted in the final verse of the hymn:

*Lord, let at last Thine angels come,
To Abram's bosom bear me home,
That I may die unfearing;
And in its narrow chamber keep
My body safe in peaceful sleep
Until Thy reappearing;*

Winston, bishop though he was, swallowed hard and strove to keep his composure.

And then from death awaken me

How many years did he have left in life?

*That these mine eyes with joy may see,
O Son of God, Thy glorious face,
My Savior and my Fount of grace.*

Winston steeled himself, as the choir boys' voices echoed heavenward once more in a descant which filled the whole cathedral:

*Lord Jesus Christ, my prayer attend, my prayer
   attend,*

And I will praise Thee without end! Amen.

That's a hard act to follow, Winston thought, as the clergy settled back in their stalls again.

A few encomiums followed. The service speedily came to an end.

Bishop Winston Arthur Attenborough II, facing the assembled throng from the high steps of the altar, pronounced the blessing.

Immediately the crucifer and incense-bearer moved from the sides of the chancel and began to lead the long clergy procession into the nave.

Just before they neared the front pews, however, ushers led Charlotte and her family down the center aisle to the narthex to greet the departing worshipers. As they did so, the organist began the final hymn. Immediately everyone arose and sang:

For all the saints who from their labors rest,
Who Thee by faith before the world confest,
Thy name, O Jesus, be forever blest,
Alleluia! Alleluia!

Winston also stood, adjusted the heavy miter, grasped his bishop's crook and began to follow the long line of clergy ahead of him.

The singing continued like a brush of angel's wings once more:

From earth's wide bounds, from ocean's farthest coast,
Through gates of pearl, streams in the countless host,
Singing to Father, Son, and Holy Ghost,
Alleluia! Alleluia!

Winston walked squarely down the center of the aisle, looking neither to the right or the left, his miter perfectly positioned, his bishop's crook elegantly shifting in pace with his long strides.

The golden evening brightens in the west

The organist put on the 32-foot stop.

Soon, soon, to faithful warriors cometh rest.

The choir boys were outdoing themselves.

Sweet is the calm of Paradise the blest.

As Winston neared the end of the nave, he saw Charlotte waiting in the narthex with her family.

Alleluia! Alleluia!

The hymn ended and the organist began a powerful Bach postlude, which thrust the people from the cathedral into the bursting sunshine in the patio outside.

But Winston waited in line with those who chose to greet Charlotte who stood quietly in a corner of the foyer.

What could he say to her? He removed his heavy miter and cradled it under his left arm. His vestments hung heavily on him, and he could feel sweat in his armpits.

What could he say?

Winston recalled what one colleague, whom he had bumped into in the cathedral office, had said the morning after one of the staff clergy had died. The old fellow had been something of a conservative, like Paul, but he was always smiling, and gave totally of himself to other people.

"Did you hear Father Preston died last night?" he had asked the priest.

"Yes," the man responded. He paused a moment and said, "He was a Christian gentleman of radiant decency."

But that was too heavy for this moment.

What would he say to Charlotte?

What was *she* thinking now?

How did she *feel* about him?

The line moved closer.

Then he remembered another friend whose father had died. Everyone had come into his office and made innocuous comments like, "I know just how you feel." He had told Winston that finally he was ready to puke.

Until one friend had stuck her head in the door, and said simply, "I care."

Charlotte was in front of him now. She was a queen. Her composure was remarkable. She looked at him steadily with her intense brown eyes.

"I care," he said.

"I know," she said.

59

The longest moment in Winston's life had passed. Then he was besieged by a battery of priests and other clergy who walked out with him into the colorful cathedral gardens.

A half an hour passed. Winston half-heard the conversations of the young priests clustered around him.

"Bishop, what is your evaluation of the dialog we've been having with the Lutherans?"

Winston began his often-quoted reply to that question.

But he was visualizing himself with Charlotte—perhaps six months from now, discreetly in the presence of other friends. Perhaps spending a classic Christmas holiday in Connecticut—after high mass at the cathedral, of course.

Memories of Barbara Stanwyck in *Christmas in Connecticut,* Bing Crosby in *Holiday Inn,* and in *White Christmas* flooded into his mind. sleigh bells, snow . . . snow . . . snow . . . SNOW!

A young priest tugged his sleeve, and his mind, back to the present.

"Canon Evans was a great saint among us, wasn't he, Bishop?"

Winston sighed, looked heavenward (inwardly groaning, wondering how to answer *that* one) and thankful his demeanor was taken as an affirmation by the awed young clergy gathered around him.

Maybe, after a year, people wouldn't talk, and he and Charlotte could be married.

In der Schweiz. In Switzerland! Honeymoon there—as close to God's heaven as one can get!

Now most of the worshipers had left. He saw Charlotte standing beside some large tree roses, quietly talking with friends.

Their eyes met again.

Memory, he thought. *It is not past, it is present.*

It is here. Now.

The years fell away.

He walked across the lawn, excusing himself quietly to the last few people gathered near her.

Charlotte's friends nodded to the bishop and walked away.

He took her hand gently.
"Charlotte," he said.
"Winston," she replied.

For Discussion

An elderly man and his wife sat in their backyard. Their children were grown and gone, the house empty. The man had just received his first retirement check in the mail.
They both looked tired.
They gazed quietly at each other.
"So this is it?" said the woman.

1. Is "The Memory" a credible story?
2. As young people or those in middle age look at people mature in years, what do they think? What are the stereotypes about "old age"? Which ones are untrue?
3. What are the most significant insights you have gained from people in their later years?
4. The bishop mused, "Memory is not the past. It is contemporary. It is the context of what I think and do *today*." What actual steps can one take to not "*live* in the past" but in the *now?*
5. From your perspective, if you had your life to live over again, would you do it differently? If so, how? What key insights do you have to share for those still in their youth?
6. An 82-year-old layman said, "The two most important things in life are modesty and a good death." What did he mean?
7. What other issues relating to aging and nearing death are the concern of members in your congregation? (Gerontological illnesses, nursing homes, retirement and finances, relation to children, etc.)
8. What does God promise older people? See Isaiah 46:4; Revelation 2:10.

9. To what lifestyle are older people called? See Ecclesiastes 12:1; Titus 2:2–5.
10. How should younger people treat those older than they are? See Leviticus 19:32; Proverbs 16:31, 23:22; 1 Timothy 5:1–2.

SESSION 6
Death/Life

The Christmas Letter

Carla looked out the window of the rented mountain cabin. Three days till Christmas. But it would be a different Christmas this year. Never the same.

Because this year Bill wouldn't be with them. Since his death in August her whole world had changed. And for the boys, too. Bud and Jerry sleeping upstairs. Rugged, boisterous teenagers. How they had loved their Dad! Uncle Frank, too.

But never again. Not this Christmas. She'd had to get away from the house in Burlingame. So they'd rented this cabin and driven up to Lake Tahoe last night. What a different Christmas this would be.

But—*no presents* this year! That she'd made very clear. Not without Bill.

Carla turned the bacon in the pan. Its appetizing smell drifted upwards in the high-lofted combination kitchen and family room. The boys and Uncle Frank would smell it and soon be down.

She gazed around the large comfortable cabin. A small mansion, really.

The motif was early 20-century American. There were old trays with the faces of women with long hair, flowered hats, and demure smiles. Old pots and pans and kitchen

utensils hung from the large beams that crisscrossed the massive, open ceiling.

A huge black metal stove dominated one side of the room in front of a ruggedly attractive brown stone wall. At the far end of the room a long stairway swept up to where the boys and Uncle Frank were still sleeping.

Carla replenished her coffee and looked out the wide window over the sink. Beyond the redwood deck were hundred foot high pines through which she could see the deep blue hues of Lake Tahoe. Over at a neighboring cabin, smoke curled lazily from a chimney.

Since their arrival the night before, five inches of fresh snow had fallen. And now, in the bright morning sun, gentle breezes puffed through the trees and shook the branches with their sparkling treasure. The snow fell like silver dust shimmering through the air far to the ground below.

"Mornin', Mom," two happy voices called from the loft.

"Good morning, boys. Breakfast's almost ready. Tell Uncle Frank."

"He's dressed and out of the bathroom. Just reading. Be right down."

Carla looked at the set table. And then at the little Christmas tree.

She hadn't wanted that this year, either.

The little Christmas tree. She'd hardly noticed it when they first walked in with their suitcases. It was an unusual "tree." It was from Scandinavia, Frank said. He'd seen them before. Made of curled and wrapped pieces of wood and shavings that formed the branches. Small multicolored lights hung on the tree. Bud had plugged them in quickly and then Mother had cautioned, "Remember!"

But it was actually a cute tree. With a scattering of paper ornaments—lions, tigers, hearts, little baskets, and clay birds from Mexico.

Carla looked quickly away from the tree and started the omelets.

"Ten minutes, guys," she called up into the rafters.

The next three days sped by. It was not as depressing as she thought it would be. It *had* been five months now. They took their usual trips—driving as far as they could up toward Angora Lakes until the snow banks stopped them.

They enjoyed relaxed evening dinners at State Line. Again they took a trip on the Dixie Queen across the lake—as they had done so often with Bill before.

They worshiped in a nearby church on Christmas Eve. And then suddenly—*Christmas morning.*

Carla stood at the stove again, this time fixing Bud and Jerry's favorite food—blueberry waffles. "Ten minutes!" she called. But this time, to her surprise, three grinning faces appeared over the stairway railing.

"Merry Christmas!" they chorused.

"Merry Christmas," Carla responded, swallowing hard.

As Bud jumped down the stairs, three steps at a time, he quickly plugged in the lights on the little tree.

"Bud . . . " Carla began.

"Love ya, Mom," he quipped. "Hey, my favorite breakfast!"

It was a quiet breakfast, but when it was over, Uncle Frank said, "I have something for you, Carla."

"But, Frank, I said *no presents* this year."

"I know. But this is from Bill."

"From *Bill,*" said Carla, wide-eyed. "But how . . . ?"

"A few weeks before he died (he knew he was going), he asked me to buy these. Just a few little things. So you would know he was still 'with' you this Christmas."

And there they were—a beautiful red Andri music box for Carla that played "Deck the Halls with Boughs of Holly" in perfect pitch. A new sweater for each of the boys. "And he bought me a new pipe," Frank concluded. "Told me to pick it out for myself."

They remained silent for a moment.

Then, "He was a great Dad," Jerry said.

"The best," Bud echoed.

Carla felt the spell of Christmas! The towering ceiling above her. The scent of fresh coffee. The little Christmas tree—all aglow now. The animal ornaments seemed to wink at her. But no presents under the tree.

She rose abruptly. "Just wait here, you," she said laughing, as she sailed up the stairs to her bedroom.

Seconds later she was back, her arms laden with gifts. "If Bill could pull a surprise, well, I can, too!"

"But, Mom" said Bud. "You said 'no presents!'"

"I know, but a mother can change her mind."

And so they unwrapped them. New sports outfits for the boys, books, posters, tapes—and a bunch of funny little things she'd picked up down at Raley's at the "Y."

Fine tobacco from Holland and a warm Scotch plaid scarf for Uncle Frank.

Carla beamed. "I just couldn't resist. After that first day here I was kinda down. But then when I was coming back from my walk two days ago I saw the tree glow in the window. Oh, I know, you unplugged it when you heard my steps on the deck. But that little tree sent a glow through me. It seemed to keep reaching out to me, its branches like the arms of an old friend."

"That's great, Mom," said Jerry.

"I'll have to admit I even turned on the tree lights when you guys were out of the house!" Carla beamed.

Bud and Jerry looked at each other with big smiles. "Our turn now," they chimed.

"What . . . ?" said Carla.

Bud bound up and down the stairs—returning with his arms full.

"Surprise! Merry Christmas!" he chortled.

"But why did you—when did you . . . ?" Carla began.

"We saw you wrapping presents in your bedroom two days ago," Jerry responded, "so we thought we could change our minds, too."

And so the unwrapping began again.

Finally, with a corporate sigh of elation, they all looked at the Christmas paper-strewn floor and grinned at each other.

Then Frank said, still smiling, "There's one thing more. Bill has a message for you."

Carla and the boys looked at him with puzzled frowns.

"You know how he planned ahead."

They nodded.

Slowly Frank took his pipe out of his mouth and reached inside his jacket for an envelope.

Opening it, he read:

A Final Letter to My Wife and Boys and Uncle Frank:

Whenever I die, please do not grieve for me. I am beyond pain—by God's grace in the presence of our Lord. You are the ones in pain. That grieves me now. But in heaven I will not know pain.

So if you hurt, I am truly sorry. But dwell on the joys—the many joyful times the Lord permitted us to have together. Christmases and Easters and birthdays and countless summer weekends by our pool—and evenings by the fireplace together.

God has been most merciful and gracious and generous to us!

I remember my parents and grandparents so well as I write this. They are present with me right now—not "dead."

Remember our common faith in our Lord and Savior Jesus Christ. He lives in our hearts. And think of me as living in your hearts and lives now, too.

So "do not sorrow as those who have no hope."

I will see you again!

I love each of you so much—each in a very special and different way.

So now rejoice! Christ is born—for us!

I will see you again!

—Dad

The four sat quietly in the large room. The fire crackled. Outside, the birds fluttered around the snowbanks searching for food.

The trees shivered. Their silver dust fluttered to the ground.

Carla spoke. "He's still with us, after all. And yet I know he's enjoying a far more joyous 'Christmas.'

"I miss Bill. We all miss him. But one day we'll all celebrate Christmas with him."

The boys and Frank nodded their assent.

A log in the fireplace snapped. The smell of bacon still permeated the air. Outside, the birds sang. The little Christmas tree glowed and glimmered and the tiny lion, tiger, and bird ornaments stared solemnly at the scene.

And so it was a good Christmas.

Not like other Christmases in the past.

But it was a good Christmas after all.

Do you know of friends with whom you would like to share this story? Why not share it, including the Appendix.

For Discussion

In a worship service a pastor had a prayer following the death of a woman who was a member of the parish. Then he turned to the congregation and said, "And now let us pray for the next one among us who will die."

Are we not only "ready to live" but also "ready to die"?

"Only one who is ready to live is ready to die. And only one who is ready to die, is ready to live."

How do you approach *your* death?

1. In the story, what were the key elements in Bill's letter to his family?
2. How do your own feelings about your death compare to Bill's approach to the end of his life?
3. Is death our friend or our enemy? Bach wrote the moving piece "Come, Sweet Death." And a hymn (*LBW* 527) speaks of death as "kind and gentle" (stanza 6). What does Scripture say? See Romans 6:23; 1 Samuel 15:32; Psalm 55:4; Matthew 26:38; 1 Corinthians 15:56; Hebrews 2:15; 2 Timothy 1:9–10.
4. How did the apostle Paul find the balance between wanting to die and wanting to live (at the same time)? See Philippians 1:21–26.
5. Is it ever wrong to pray for death to come?
6. What specific plans should one make for one's own death without becoming morbid or obsessed about it?
7. Let's review our basic questions as we've considered these stories:

    a. *Is the story true to life or not? Give reasons for your answer.*

    Do you know of people who, like Bill, have "set their house in order" toward the end of their life?

b. *What, if anything, does the story have to say to our Christian faith and life?*

"The Christian lives as an exile from our heavenly home. Therefore there is a certain detachment from this world, and yet a zest and vividness at the same time, knowing we shall pass this way but once."

Do you agree with this statement? If so, how does one achieve such a life-style (by God's grace, of course!)? See Psalm 1:2, 90:12, 118:24.

c. *How does [the story] reveal or point to our need? (Law.)*

A young husband's wife was stricken with cancer and she faced a bilateral mastectomy. "This removes the veil of immortality we feel at youth," he wrote a friend.

What do you see as the key forces which can detract a person from being "ready to live—ready to die"? See Galatians 5:19–25; 1 John 2:15–18.

d. *How does (the story) point to or suggest God's action for us in Christ? (Gospel)*

What was the focal point of Bill's faith? See Exodus 34:6; John 14:19; Hebrews 12:1–2.

See the Appendix for a follow-up for "The Christmas Letter."

APPENDIX

For use as a follow-up to the story, "The Christmas Letter."*

For this family "it was a good Christmas after all." But only because they knew the comforting certainty that their loved one was "with the Lord." And they would see him again—upon their resurrection.

Is that certitude and hope yours? Christ promises that "whoever lives and believes in Me will never die." When we confess our sins, and trust totally in Christ's death on the cross *for us,* then we have forgiveness and the confidence of having eternal life.

But Christianity is not just for the hereafter. Christ brings comfort to us in present sorrow, pain, and loneliness. He is a reality now—or He can be in your life when you seek Him. He is ready to be revealed more personally to you in His Word and in the fellowship of the church.

Christians are not perfect people but sinners like everyone else. And they will welcome you to their caring community and share the peace Jesus wants you to have in your life.

If you have someone with whom you would like to share the Christian faith, talk to your pastor or write Christian Service Center, The Lutheran Laymen's League, 2185 Hampton Avenue, St. Louis, MO, 63139-2983. *Or phone 1-800-7-LAYMEN.*

ACKNOWLEDGMENTS

Session 1

"The Bright Red Sports Car" appeared originally as "The Bright Red T-Bird in *This Day* 14:12 (August 1963), copyright 1963 by Concordia Publishing House. All rights reserved.

"Talking about . . . Where Is God?" is from *The Lutheran Witness* 108:1 (January 1989). Copyright © 1989 by Donald L. Deffner.

Session 3

"Hello, Jan" is from *Please Change Me, God,* by Donald L. Deffner. Copyright © 1986 by Concordia Publishing House. All rights reserved.

Session 6

"The Christmas Letter" appeared originally in *The Lutheran Witness* 107:12 (December 1988), copyright © 1988 by Donald L. Deffner.

Some of the prayers are from *Come Closer to Me, God!* by Donald L. Deffner. Copyright 1982 by Donald L. Deffner. All rights reserved.

Also, my thanks go to David Owren, Tracey Blanchard, Peter Garrison, Dirk van der Linde, Mary Ann Berry, Margaret J. Anderson, Jan Sheldon, Gloria Smallwood, Micheal Kroll, Jeffrey Walther, Becky Kieschnick, Jessica Wilmarth, and Earl Gaulke.